Odd Oddyssey
of the
"Wise Xerxes"

Odd Oddyssey
of the
"Wise Xerxes"

Aleister Ejazi

Charleston, SC
www.PalmettoPublishing.com

Odd Oddyssey of The "Wise Xerxes"

Copyright © 2021 by Aleister Ejazi

All rights reserved

No portion of this book may be reproduced, stored in a retrieval system, or transmitted in any form by any means–electronic, mechanical, photocopy, recording, or other–except for brief quotations in printed reviews, without prior permission of the author.

First Edition

Paperback ISBN: 978-1-63837-336-0
eBook ISBN: 978-1-63837-337-7

PREFACE

What you about to read contains material that may be considered too graphic for certain readers by many. This is purely for entertainment purposes only. All this is about the "Wise Xerxes" and the "Goddess Armodusia" in a fictional manner and details are greatly exaggerated.

Legends speak of a skeletal warrior with glowing minty eyes and nostrils that lived about 6,000 or 10,000 years ago. This was the "Wise Xerxes". It all began when he joined the "Order of the Black Fire". Such an organization greatly angered the "Goddess Armodusia".

She secretly influenced the rotting warrior to go in search of cursed objects by showing him her "coconuts" of truth. It was then that all was clear to the "Wise Xerxes".

He began heading for such objects in the sexy Suggestive Cave. To get to this cave, he had to climb the Mountain of Hallucination. This mountain took the form of a female torso. The navel cavity lies the entrance of the cave. The mountain was so glorious, the "Wise Xerxes" looked upon it for several days.

On his way up the mountain, the "Wise Xerxes" was startled at the sight of a blind cyclops. As he prepared for battle, the one eyed giant convinced him that she was vegan. It took him 24 hours to realize that cyclopses simply do not exist. Cyclopses are also known to eat humans and not crops.

Later, the most ungraceful unicorn trotted towards him. As he was about to flee from the ugly beast, the "Wise Xerxes" slowly realized that unicorns were beautiful and they hated all men. The irritated rotting warrior turned back to resume climbing. He has just hallucinated twice now.

As the "Wise Xerxes" was about to enter the sexy Suggestive Cave, he noticed a rather funny scent. Now things are really getting stupid. The mountain's navel smells just like a navel. This was another hallucination and a very clever one too.

Once in the cave, the "Wise Xerxes" spotted a silver leprechaun and chased it for days before a mirror caught his attention. Then it struck him that leprechauns are green. Upon looking at the mirror, he saw himself in the bare flesh for the first time and accidently broke the mirror by posing in it.

That mirror was obviously the Mirror of Nudity. This was the sexy Suggestive Cave for a reason. It was decorated with arousing imagery on the walls. Where else would the Mirror of Nudity be?

If only the "Wise Xerxes" had known that it was the Mirror of Nudity then he might have never went near it as the Mirror of Nudity only works on those that are not already naked. The mirror's purpose was to be the guardian of all things sexy.

The once sexy planet Sexerea has been morphed badly into the appalling planet Prudaria. This ended up giving the "Order of the Black Fire" complete control of the planet. For some reason, the "Goddess Armodusia" was quite calm. She just created extra cursed objects and placed them on the planet's green moon.

Upon his arrival, the humiliated warrior found himself in a forest of buttocks. There were buttocks everywhere. He has been mooned like he has never been mooned before. He spent a month wandering the place.

Eventually, the "Wise Xerxes" finds a fleshy key. It has blood on it and the bow is like a bull's head. What could it possibly unlock?

Hours later, the "Wise Xerxes" stood before a grand heart shaped lock. It was then that he realized that the key was the cursed Bull Key. That is one cursed object down. There is supposedly one other one in the area.

Once the "Wise Xerxes" shoved the cursed Bull Key right up the heart shaped lock, he went from a rotting skeletal warrior to a sexy war maiden wearing nothing but a bra and panties. This was the reason the "Goddess Armodusia" was quite calm earlier. In the distance stood a grand altar. A sword rested beyond it. The hilt was stainless steel and the blade was an unbreakable crystal.

As the now war maiden pulls out the sword from its rather scary pedestal, she gets a rather sensationally orgasmic feeling while being penetrated by the darkness of the "Goddess Armodusia". Suddenly the sexy warrior notices that she is clad in armour. It was only then that she saw an inscription on the altar that read "Only sexy maidens may enter here.". That explained the sex change.

Upon her arrival, the sexy warrior realized that the sword and armour were the other cursed objects back at the green moon. The sword was the Sword of Paradise which would restore the planet to its former sexual glory but with a twist and the armour was the Armour of Desire which morphs into whatever is necessarily seductive at the moment. In order to make the planet sexy again, the sexy war maiden had to dance around naked with the Sword of Paradise. The twist of this turned out to be the Mountain of Hallucination being replaced and all creatures imagined becoming real.

So, the sexy warrior returns to where the Mountain of Hallucination used to be but is halted by nothing more than H2O. The sexy warrior saw that she had no choice but to swim to proceed any further.

On the horizon, she saw a metallic island. This was Steel Island. As she began searching for more cursed objects, the sexy warrior was suddenly enticed by two naked twin sisters that were enticed by the overwhelming scent of coconuts.

The twins both had lovely purple hair, red glowing eyes, and buttocks resembling the heart shaped lock. What was that about an overwhelming scent of the holy crop? There were none to be found until the sexy warrior saw that the Armour of Desire morphed into a Cocokini which was a bikini made from coconuts. Talk about a holy bikini.

After introductions were made, the twins informed the sexy war maiden that there were 10 cursed objects on the island but they desired 2 of them. All the twins asked of the sexy warrior was for her to be their mistress.

They can keep the cursed objects that they desired this way so, the sexy warrior took the role of a mistress.

The trio began searching for the first cursed object. It was the Diamond of Faith which rested on the back of a very bulky turtle. The beast could only be found near the beach. So, the trio looked for days with no luck. Suddenly, a green skinned humanoid figure leaped through the trees ahead.

The twins had a feeling they knew the identity of the figure. When the figure found, killed, and dragged the beast away, the twins were 100% sure of the figure's identity. They informed their mistress of a dangerous huntress with green skin and golden eyes that is said to be the most skilled huntress of all and she possesses the Diamond of Faith. They also informed their mistress that the huntress is also said to be a nymphomaniac.

So, the trio went after the huntress in hopes of fulfilling her sexual fantasies and retrieve the Diamond of Faith. The huntress made a blouse out of the turtle's skin before she saw the trio in the trees ahead. She took off her silver thong panties begging the trio to do what they came to do. She can read minds apparently.

Sensing that their mistress is quite tense due to being a virgin, the twins assured her that they can get the Diamond of Faith for her. As they hip swayed towards the huntress, she stripped completely naked.

Sexy time began with a good French kissing session. Then the twins ended up getting a good long spanking and poking. In appreciation, the twins discharged silver and made the huntress discharge gold by means of a long rough humping and mouth to buttocks action.

Suddenly, the Armour of Desire morphed into a tight undershirt and leggings along with the thong panties and strapless lace bandeau bra that the sexy warrior was put in since the sex change. The timing could not have been better considering that the sexy warrior decided to get in on the action. None of the girls could believe how sexy the war maiden was at the moment. They each lowered her leggings and thong panties to take turns giving her a much better spanking. The sexy warrior could not believe how pink her buttocks was.

After spanking her, the other girls poked her every hole except the ones on her head and kissed as well as licked her on the same exact areas. To finish her off, the other girls French kissed her while fondling her "coconuts".

The sexy war maiden seductively lifted her thong panties and leggings back up and asked to have the Diamond of Faith to which the huntress agreed. The huntress thanked the trio for giving her the best night of her life and begged for another if they met once more to which the trio agreed.

After departing the lair of the huntress, the trio heard loud whining at the seashore. It turned out to be a shiny mermaid who was searching for her plesiosaur "Ass". An ass is a donkey. Why name a plesiosaur "Ass"?

So, the search for "Ass" began but the beast was nowhere to be found on the beach. Plus, the trio felt really foolish going around and calling out "Ass". As the Armour of Desire went back to being the holy bikini, the trio went deep into the sea. It did not take long to find the beast.

It was at Davy Jones's Locker swimming in circles the whole time. The beast might as well be an ass. Also, what kind of mermaid would not go look for something in her own domain? For whatever reason, "Ass" swam willingly towards the trio. The trio rode the beast back to the mermaid who explained how the Diamond of Faith works.

Apparently, the Diamond of Faith draws in the faith of beasts. The mermaid thanked the trio by presenting 2 bikinis to them. The cursed objects desired by the twins is finally theirs. One bikini was a Steelkini forged from the island's cursed steel. The other bikini was a Jewelrkini crafted from the island's cursed jewels.

Upon being rewarded, the twins begged their mistress to model the bikinis to which she agreed. They then began rubbing and kissing her all over. Once the twin donned the bikinis, they became the Bikini Sisters.

That very evening, the Bikini Sisters took their mistress to meet another mistress who was a vampiress. The trio went to the center of the island where an aluminum foil palace stood.

As they entered, the Armour of Desire morphed into a tank top and skirt. In the great hall, the vampiress was on the floor dying.

Unlike others of her kind, the vampiress sucked blood out of the buttocks and "coconuts". So, the sexy warrior took her skirt off and bent over so that the vampiress could feed.

The vampiress slowly rose up and sank her fangs into the sexy warrior's spanked buttocks. The Bikini Sisters joined their mistress in nursing the other mistress back to health by offering their own "coconuts" and the vampiress sank her fangs in each one.

Due to their generosity, the trio temporarily became undead. The vampiress could not believe how tender they were that they did not let her die. In appreciation, she took the trio in and even dined with them for the time being. Then she led them down a secret passage for some vampiric sexy time.

The Bikini Sisters and both mistresses got naked and embraced each other like there was no tomorrow. Then they ended up fanging and spanking each other on the buttocks, "coconuts", and sex organs. Last thing to do was to poke each other everywhere from the neck down. It was sure a night to remember for all eternity.

The next night, the girls discussed the cursed objects to which the vampiress informed the trio that 2 of them were in her crypt. They turned out to be an extra pointy boomerang and a golden skull. The boomerang was the Boomerang of Chaos and the skull was the Skull of Wealth. With the skull, one can never run out of silver fahlavis. With the boomerang, one can spread chaos wherever desired.

Rich with the planet's currency and armed with chaos, the trio set their sights on the other cursed objects. Before departing, the vampiress winked and promised that they will meet once more.

Back on the beach, the trio encountered a rather pesky frog the size of each girl. The trio saw that the beast was wearing one of the cursed objects on its head. That explained the constant talking.

The beast was wearing the Circlet of Rumors which causes one to spread random rumors. Once the trio had enough of the beast, they killed it with their buttocks and took the circlet in their possession. Just as the trio were about to seek refuge, their vampiress nights ended.

Suddenly, a massive serpent rose from the waves and swallowed the trio. Inside the serpent, the trio started to panic until the serpent told them that they will not be digested. Oddly enough, the serpent sounded like the huntress.

If the serpent is indeed the huntress then she certainly has been swallowing some strange things for a while. There were clothes, jewelry, and even things that would be used for sexual activities like spankings.

Just then, the Bikini Sister with the jeweled bikini came across a beautifully crafted shield while the other Bikini Sister came across a beautifully forged dagger before a scorpion the size of the frog killed by the trio came along and upskirted their mistress.

Compelled by their bikinis, they armed themselves with paddles and bent their mistress over as she took her skirt off to be paddled.

As she discharged silver, the sexy warrior moaned and begged for more. As their mistress ordered, the Bikini Sisters paddled her until she discharged bronze. After embracing, the sexy warrior got on her bare hands and knees for even more paddling and then humping. To finish her off, both girls French kissed and rubbed their mistress all over which caused her to discharge gold. This must be how the huntress feels at times.

As the trio picked up the shield and dagger, the serpent tossed them up like a salad in the middle of a jungle. In the far distance, a fire breathing silverchest came up to the trio. These apes are usually combative but this one was quite calm due to the Diamond of Faith. It ended up leading the trio to a grand temple and grunted "FOOD". It must have been ravenous.

To get into the temple, a slit and a hole had to be filled in. The Bikini Sister with the shield sexually placed it in the hole while the other thrusted the dagger sexually in the slit. As the temple's door opened, the Bikini Sisters poofed out of existence and left their bikinis behind.

Of course, that is why the beast grunted "FOOD".

The temple was indeed a food temple, the shield was the Shield of Guilt, and the dagger was the Dagger of Peace. Only those that are guilty of something and enter in peace can enter.

It was burgers, fries, hot dogs, and chicken galore within the temple's walls. However, the altar was defiled with bones and unfinished meals. What savages blasphemed food like that?

To restore the holiness, the sexy warrior had to clear away the bones and prepare the quiche and pizza of divine darkness to place on the altar. As she finished eating, the sexy warrior realized some of the bones were cursed Chicken Bones of Doom.

As she grasped the cursed bones, the sexy warrior got tossed into the Canyon of Wisdom where she realized the sausages that she used were the cursed Hellish Sausages.

Thanks to the cursed bones, the sexy warrior's flesh rotted away. The now bony warrior must seek the Fountain of Idiocy to find the Ass of Destiny.

After days of searching, she reached the fountain. However, the beast was nowhere to be seen. The only things in sight was the fountain along with its corrupt purple waters until she noticed a tarnished copper lamp floating on the fountain's waters.

A lamp is a lamp regardless of how it looks. That is what the bony warrior thought until she saw that the lamp was all used up. As she wildly tossed the lamp around like a monkey, an angry jinn popped out of the lamp to see what the ruckus was about.

Seeing the petrified bony warrior, the sexy jinn knew exactly what to do. She made a hunky man out of the bony warrior which caused him to pop out of what he had on. After gawking stupidly, she shoved a Buffalo Burger of Glory in his mouth which morphed the ruined outfit and caged him from head to toe in silver. After wrestling and spanking each other, the now shiny warrior shoved the jinn back in the lamp and returned the lamp to the fountain.

As night fell, a wolf howled at the planet's green moon as a floral back spider enticed the shiny warrior with her long legs and escorted him to a very beautifully painted belt

It was the Iron Belt of Death. The 8 legged beast spun some special sexy web to weave a bag, pulled the other cursed objects out of the shiny warrior's buttocks, and tossed the filled bag to him. As the beast left, the shiny warrior noticed a trail of blood.

He followed the trail for days before he realized that he was going in circles. He began ranting like a lunatic until he discovered some amusing objects which were a skull ax that attracts body snatchers, a blood stained ocarina that drives all insane, and a glow in the dark crystal hammer that blinds all that dare activate its powers which only the leaders of the "Order of the Black Fire" can do.

Soon, the shiny warrior found himself in a beautifully deadly garden which was the source of the trail all along. Deep in the garden grew the legendary bleeding gem fruits.

Not only are these mouthwatering crops the most delicious, they are also the most noxious. They launch heads from bodies and blows them up as one headless suitsman found out the hard way.

Only love eagles can feast upon them. They do it since it is the only way to lay the legendary bleeding gem eggs which hatches worlds but none have ever hatched. Other dangers awaited the shiny warrior.

Bronze roses gave men fellatios of death. He was surrounded by the titillated flowers which were all gawking stupidly at his shiny erection.

As the lips of the roses came closer, red glowing eyes from the darkness chased the shiny warrior out of the garden. It was a grudge kitty that later claimed to have known him since he was born. He ends up pouncing on the feline while crying "Papa" to which the feline responds "I am your mama you idiot." while dragging the shiny warrior by the legs kicking and screaming to the Desert of Agelessness where the last cursed objects are.

The sands of this desert lived many earth eels. These beasts shock the youth out of others when the desert's sands freezes them in their youth.

He wandered around for a long while until he ended up with a foot wedged in his shiny buttocks. It was then that the shiny warrior realized that the grudge kitty was gone and that the foot wedged in his shiny buttocks belonged to a body snatcher lured in by the skull ax.

The ageless hermit threw down his helmet and his gauntlets and started savagely spanking the shiny warrior in order to get his foot out of the shiny warrior's buttocks. When it was obvious that the ageless hermit's foot was not coming out of the shiny warrior's buttocks, the shiny warrior ended up leaving the ageless hermit without a boot. To add insult to injury, the shiny warrior stole the ageless hermit's helmet and gauntlets as well before tickling him to death.

The shiny warrior soon found himself in a pit of earth eels that were "busy" with their queen Armadeus. Once discovered, the shiny warrior cowered with his buttocks in the air which still had the boot stuck in it. All the subject earth eels died laughing at the very sight of a boot stuck in the shiny warrior's buttocks.

With all her subjects dead, Armadeus went to shock the shiny warrior but ended up just shocking the boot in his buttocks which gave a smell so bad that it made the earth eel queen gag. While gagging, a crazy swan came out of nowhere and swallowed her.

Then the feathered freak chased the shiny warrior to the end of the desert which was blocked by winged swine and white desert monkeys. To get passed all the beasts, the shiny warrior pooted so hard that they all fell dead and the boot was finally out.

Out of the desert, the shiny warrior found himself in a land of fire and magma. Before he had a chance to look around, the shiny warrior got smacked in the face by a skull shaped lantern tossed at him. He bent down to pick it up and got spanked with such force. He got up with a major erection only to get flogged across his buttocks and later caned.

As aroused as he was, the shiny warrior had things to do like find his spanker which turned out to be a lovely transgender cyborg dominatrix who goes by "Mistress Karma".

The kinky nuclear haired cyborg did not take long to talk naughty to the shiny warrior before spanking his buttocks again while some lava mummies watched thinking "Karma is one cruel mistress.". Then she spanked his hands, feet, and erect penis after pulling a tiny pair of panties right up his buttocks. To finish him off, she drilled into his anus after tearing off his panties and then she rammed her penis drill in his mouth.

For the whole ordeal, she demanded that he worship her from her head to her toes and then propose to her. As he offered his helmet and gauntlets in marriage, she ended up rejecting him and falling apart in the worst way possible.

While mourning the death of his mistress, the shiny warrior realized that the helmet and gauntlets were the last cursed objects that he was sent to find. The gauntlets were the Gauntlets of Discipline which explained why he got spanked, wedgied, drilled, forced to worship, and forced to propose. The helmet was the Helmet of Desecration which explained his mistress falling apart.

When he went to pick up the lantern, the last of the cursed objects, and parts of his mistress, the shiny warrior discovered that he was somehow pregnant and the Ass of Destiny randomly came to his aid by carrying him and his things until he was no longer with child. Before he could mount the Ass of Destiny, the shiny warrior had his buttocks spanked after getting his buttocks humped and probed.

The "Order of the Black Fire" found out about his shenanigans and so, they robbed him of all he had. To make matters worse, he went into labor.

Lucky for him, a bunch of lava mummies arrived to help him give birth. They dug their filthy bandaged hands deep inside him and pulled out an ugly cyborg baby which they adopted and named Dick.

As the now naked warrior was about to go after the "Order of the Black Fire", every volcano in the land blew him sky high burning him badly which restored him to his original state and placed him on Captain Spanker's ship.

Captain Spanker and her band of pirates were the sexiest pirates in history. They told the "Wise Xerxes" that they were willing to help him get his booty back if he helped them fish for 2 sea beasts.

As he looked at his tailbone and thought of the benefits, Captain Spanker and her spankee crew facepalmed and explained what they meant by booty. He ended up helping them anyway because why not?

The first sea beast was Octobaba. They all found the giant horned octopus that squirts invisible ink off the coast of Hun Hun Bun Bun where it was taken hostage before it had a chance to ink, spank, or even anally probe anyone.

Using Octobaba as bait, they all circled Hun Hun Bun Bun until the great frozen shark Perky chased them, got tired, and cut into ice cubes.

With Perky gone, they all milked Octobaba for all his invisible ink before plucking his horns to use as weapons and eating the rest of him.

After thanking him for aiding them fish for the 2 sea beasts, Captain Spanker and her spankee crew got the "Wise Xerxes" drunk on coconut rum before firing him out of a cannon right past Hun Hun Bun Bun and into the Poison Maze Swamp. The swamp's air made all in it reek of beasts until they ended up becoming beasts.

With only a year left, the "Wise Xerxes" wandered aimlessly through the swamp before crying himself to sleep. He woke up days later with a panda's buttocks pressed so firmly on him. Talk about a crushed pelvis.

The panda turned out to be the planet's odor master. It seems that the stink munchies have returned for their 69th spring cleaning and these crocodilian neat freaks need to be stopped which is where the odor master and the planet's only stench agency "B.O." comes in to rid the planet of all that is neat and clean.

There was only one for such a mess free case. He was "B.O."'s smelliest agent. No beast stank more than Double 0 Chicken. He and the "Wise Xerxes" went forth with "Operation Pollution" which was a botched plot to dump nuclear muck all over the swamp.

The stink munchies wiped out "B.O." while the "Wise Xerxes" fled with the aid with a mime to Hun Hun Bun Bun where a bunch of honey covered bunnies called hunny bunnies lived with their large and seductive bee partners.

It was said that a giant serpentine creature with the power to turn mortals into expensive statues named Armodeus lived in Hun Hun Bun Bun's crystal cave.

Upon his arrival, the "Wise Xerxes" soiled himself out of fear and then drooled with greed at the sight of all that dared to face the rich stare of Armodeus. He figured that he would honor the victims by breaking them up and keeping the chunks along with a crystal ball and crystal egg.

Once the two met, Armodeus vowed revenge on the "Wise Xerxes" for the death of his wife Armadeus when it was a crazy swan that killed her. After their blind encounter, the "Wise Xerxes" blinded Armodeus with the crystal ball and crystal egg. He then ran laughing out of the crystal cave to hunt down the "Order of the Black Fire".

He headed to the planet's most sugary mountain known as Mount Blood Sugar where an erotic voice called out to the badly burned warrior to crawl on all fours up the mountain.

While working up the chocolatey foot of the mountain, the "Wise Xerxes" saw a thong shaped mirror in the distance. The thong shaped mirror ended up being the huntress.

She confessed to stalking the badly burned warrior since she left him in the middle of the jungle of Steel Island after swallowing him as a massive serpent which explained a lot.

Once at the creamy snow point of the mountain, the vampiress and pirates joined the two for the final battle. The mountain's snow brought all things to life which was helpful in many ways.

The closer that the odd bunch got, they were more convinced that the "Order of the Black Fire" was no more and the igloo lodge of the organization was in ruins which confirmed everything. The only thing left was the Black Fire.

The corpses of the organization's members and the cursed objects all over the place let out the fact that the "Order of the Black Fire" caused their own demise with everything they took from the "Wise Xerxes".

At last, the "Order of the Black Fire" paid the price for spreading weird ideas like the answer to everything is 42 when it is known that 2+2 is not 42 and who is named 42?

This day was honored with 3 creamy snowwomen. As for Armodeus, he felt the Black Fire nearby which he mistook for the "Wise Xerxes" and went SNAP CRACKLE POP.

The

End

OR IS IT?

HEHEHAHAHAHAHAHAHAHA

ABOUT THE AUTHOR

Born in Iran, he grew up in Los Angeles where he discovered that he had a natural talent for comedy. At the age of 19, he used his knowledge of ancient lore and modern science to put together a faith in hopes of ridding the world of silly superstition. However, his faith lacked mythology. So, he used his comedy skills and knowledge to put together the fantasy comedy: The Odd Odyssey of The "Wise Xerxes".

www.ingramcontent.com/pod-product-compliance
Ingram Content Group UK Ltd.
Pitfield, Milton Keynes, MK11 3LW, UK
UKHW061645240426
12048UKWH00033B/93